A GIFT FOR

Mom

FROM

Kaitlyn & Matthew
May 13, 2007

BELIEVE & ACHIEVE
Inspiration for the Journey Called Life

Copyright © 2004
Hallmark Licensing, Inc.

Published by Gift Books from Hallmark, a division of Hallmark Cards, Inc.
Kansas City, MO 64141
Visit us on the Web at www.Hallmark.com.

Editorial development: Jane-Elyse Pryor
Design: UDG | DesignWorks, Sisters, Oregon

Contributing writers: Ellen Brenneman, Ed Cunningham,
Eileen Drummond, Renee Duvall, Linda Elrod, Ginnie Job, Cheryl Hawkinson,
Barbara Loots, Diana Manning, Linda Staten

Printed and bound in China

BOK5108

Inspiration for the Journey Called Life

Believe
& Achieve

GIFT BOOKS
from Hallmark

As you journey through life,
choose your destinations well,
but do not hurry there.
You will arrive soon enough.
Wander the back roads
and forgotten paths,
keeping your destination
in your heart
like the fixed point of a compass.

Seek out new voices, strange sights, and ideas.

Such things are riches for the soul...

And if, upon arrival,
you find that your destination
is not exactly as you had dreamed,
do not be disappointed.
Think of all you would have missed
but for the journey there,
and know that the true worth
of your travels
lies not in where you come to be
at journey's end,
but in who you come to be
along the way.

—LINDA STATEN

Beginnings are

With courage greater
than your fear,

jump into
the unknown and
you will fly!

Dreams

take time,

patience, sustained effort,

and a willingness to fail

if they are ever to be anything more
than dreams.

The miracle of creativity

is that each of us brings

something beautiful to the world,

something no one else

has to offer.

[To believe you can is everything.]

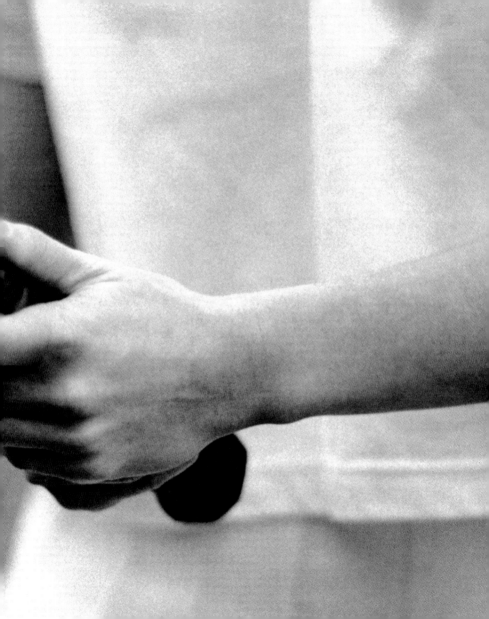

As long as we

believe in these—

unbounded possibilities,

horizons we have yet to greet

and friends that we have yet to meet,

in roads that we have yet to take

and differences we've yet to make,

in songs still waiting to be sung—

our hearts will stay forever young.

The true name of eternity is

Today.

—Philo

Today you stand on a
mountaintop...
behind you are all the
struggles and challenges
you conquered on the way;
before you lies a new
horizon filled with exciting

possibilities.

Today you choose the
direction of your life.

Sometimes all that stands

between you and the

ride of
a lifetime

is simply getting in the saddle

and seeing what you're made of.

Dream, Explore...

Discover.

The journey of a thousand miles

begins with

one step.

—Chinese Proverb

Each life needs its own...

quiet place.

Learning is a

lifetime journey...

growing older merely adds

experience to knowledge and

wisdom to curiosity.

—C. E. Lawrence

Think Big...

And if that doesn't work...

Think

Bigger!

We find in life...

exactly what we put into it.   –EMERSON

[Do what you love!]

Life is not a problem to be solved
but reality to be experienced.

– KIERKEGAARD

The stars exist
that we might know
how high
our dreams can
soar.

Sometimes

life is like a puzzle

with some of the pieces

missing.

You have to color

outside the lines

once in a while

if you want to make your life...

a masterpiece.

To live your life in your own way...

to reach for the goals you

have set for yourself...

to be the you that you want to be—

that is success.

Life is...

PLAN
B

A dream come true

is just a tough little wish

that won't take **NO** for an answer.

Life is improvisation.

Play it by ear.

Nothing

reaches higher

than the

human spirit.

Listen to your heart
and you will *fly.*

Our feet are earthbound,

but our hearts and our minds

have wings.

Dream what you dare to dream.

Go where you want to go.

Be what you want to be.

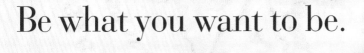

TEN THINGS TO MAKE BESIDES MONEY

time

merry

do

sense

peace

room

waves

amends

love

believe

Life
is for laughing, dancing, crying,
wondering, asking, searching, trying.

Life
is for finding, loving, losing,
exploring, daring, thinking, choosing.

Life
is for sharing, taking, giving,
creating, relating—

Life is for living!

A single dream…

can launch the journey of a lifetime.

Celebrate

where you've been,

where you're going,

and the love of life

that inspires you to grow

your whole life through.

All
it takes is
all you've
got!